4/2014

Smithsonian

LITTLE EXPLORER

HURRICANES

by Martha E. H. Rustad

CAPSTONE PRESS
a capstone imprint

Little Explorer is published by Capstone Press,
1710 Roe Crest Drive, North Mankato, Minnesota 56003
www.capstonepub.com

For Leif, my budding meteorologist. —MEHR

Library of Congress Cataloging-in-Publication Data
Cataloging-in-publication information is on file with the Library
of Congress.
ISBN 978-1-4765-3932-4 (library binding)
ISBN 978-1-4765-5180-7 (paperback)
ISBN 978-1-4765-5268-2 (paper over board)

Editorial Credits
Kristen Mohn, editor; Sarah Bennett, designer; Marcie Spence,
media researcher; Danielle Ceminsky, production specialist

Our very special thanks to Andrew K. Johnston, Geographer,
Center for Earth and Planetary Studies, National Air and Space
Museum, Smithsonian Institution, for his curatorial review.
Capstone would also like to thank Kealy Wilson, Smithsonian
Institution Project Coordinator and Product Development
Manager, and the following at Smithsonian Enterprises: Ellen
Nanney, Licensing Manager; Brigid Ferraro, Director of Licensing;
Carol LeBlanc, Senior Vice President, Consumer & Education
Products.

Image Credits
Alamy: Mike Hill, cover; AP Photo: 24 (bottom); Capstone Studio:
Karon Dubke, 7 (bottom); Getty Images: Buyenlarge, 22 (top left),
Express Newspapers, 24 (top), FPG/Hulton Archive, 22 (top
right), Michael Boccieri, 17, Robert Nickelsberg, 13 (top); NASA:
23 (top); NOAA: 27 (top), NASA, 26 (top); Newscom: Heinrich
Schoeneich/EPA, 25, John Angelillo/UPI, 16, (top), Kelly Owen/
ZUMA Press, 7 (top), 27 (bottom), Kyle Niemi – U.S. Coast Guard
via CNP, 21, NASA KRT, 14 (bottom), Sean Gardner/Reuters,
26 (bottom); Shutterstock: A Cotton Photo, 8, Alexkava, design
element, Alhovik, design element, Anton Oparin, 16 (bottom),
B747, 4-5, BlueRingMedia, 12, brickrena, 26 (back), Carolina K.
Smith MD, cover (map), 1, (map), file404, design element, Glynnis
Jones, 23 (middle), Guido Amrein, Switzerland, 10-11, 32, irabel8,
19, Leonard Zhukovsky, 23 (bottom), 29 (bottom), Lightspring,
5 (right), lukeruk, design element, Lisa F. Young, 28 (top), Mark
Winfrey, 28 (bottom), Mechanik, 14-15, Nejron Photo, 1, Pattie
Steib, 22 (bottom), Pierdelune, 9, razlomov, 4, 6, SeanPavonePhoto,
29 (top), Sharon Silverman Boyd, 18-19, Svetlana Prikhnenko,
design element, TyBy, design element, Vectomart, design element,
Vladislav Gurfinkel, 13 (bottom), 14, (top), 30-31, Yes – Royalty
Free, design element, Zacarias Pereira de Mata, 5 (left)

Printed in the United States of America in Stevens Point, Wisconsin.
092013   007769WZS14

TABLE OF CONTENTS

WHAT IS A HURRICANE?

Wild winds blow. Heavy rains pour down.

People move to safe places. What is happening? A hurricane is coming.

WHAT ARE HURRICANES CALLED AROUND THE WORLD?

If they form in the ...	people call them ...
Atlantic or eastern Pacific Oceans	hurricanes
southwestern Pacific or Indian Oceans	cyclones
northwestern Pacific Ocean	typhoons

Hurricanes are gigantic spinning storms.
They form over oceans. They travel
slowly. Sometimes they move over land.
Hurricane winds can rip up trees.

HOW HURRICANES START

A hurricane forms over very warm ocean waters. It begins as a small thunderstorm. The storm is called a tropical disturbance.

Warm waters feed energy into the storm. The storm grows. It is now called a tropical depression.

Not all tropical disturbances and depressions turn into hurricanes. The temperature, wind, and air pressure must be just right.

WHAT IS AIR PRESSURE?

It may seem light, but the air around Earth presses against us.

Meteorologists measure the pressure.

High pressure means few changes to the weather. Low pressure often brings storms.

Hurricanes grow around low-pressure air systems.

ACTIVITY!

AIR PRESSURE CHANGES

1. Find an empty plastic bottle with a screw top.

2. Fill it about one-quarter full with very hot water.

3. Screw on the lid. Let it sit for one hour.

What happened? Hot water made the air pressure inside the bottle go up. As the water and air cooled, the air pressure went down. The low air pressure made the bottle crumple in. The water temperature changed the air.

A GROWING STORM

The tropical depression builds slowly. The storm pulls more ocean water up into it. More rain falls. Winds become stronger.

The storm begins to spin around a calm center. Over a few days the storm changes. Some storms die out. Others grow stronger.

STORM SPEED

Kind of Storm	Wind Speed
tropical disturbance	up to 22 miles (35 kilometers) per hour
tropical depression	23 to 38 miles (37 to 61 km) per hour
tropical storm	39 to 73 miles (63 to 117 km) per hour
hurricane	at least 74 miles (119 km) per hour

tropical disturbance

tropical depression

tropical storm

hurricane

The tropical depression may become a tropical storm.

The tropical storm may then grow into a hurricane.

PARTS OF A HURRICANE

From above, a hurricane looks like a huge doughnut.

The **EYE** is the circle at the center. It is a calm area with slower winds.

The outer **ARMS** of the storm spiral out.

The **EYEWALL** is the strongest part of the storm. The winds are fastest here.

ON THE MOVE

Winds inside the hurricane spin and spin.

Winds outside the hurricane push the storm. They steer the storm across the ocean.

The spinning of Earth causes hurricanes to spin different directions in the two hemispheres.

In the Northern Hemisphere hurricanes spin counterclockwise.

In the Southern Hemisphere hurricanes spin clockwise.

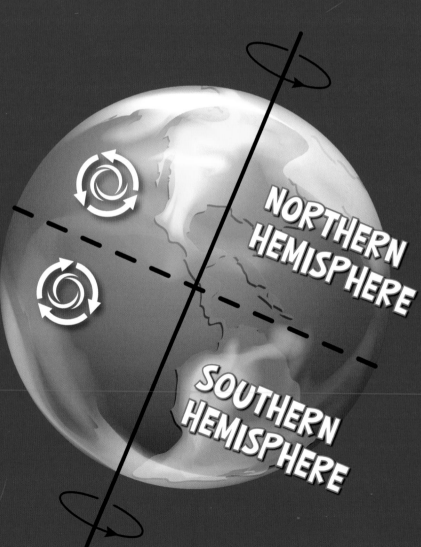

NORTHERN HEMISPHERE

SOUTHERN HEMISPHERE

The Saffir-Simpson Hurricane Wind Scale estimates possible damage from hurricane winds.

Category		Wind Speed
1		74 to 95 mph (119 to 153 km/h)
2		96 to 110 mph (154 to 177 km/h)
3		111 to 129 mph (178 to 208 km/h)
4		130 to 156 mph (209 to 251 km/h)
5		157 mph (252 km/h) or higher

Outside winds push hurricanes at about 20 miles (32 km) per hour.

HOW BIG?

Most hurricanes are about 200 miles (322 km) across.

They are about 6 to 9 miles (10 to 15 km) tall.

Very tall clouds called hot towers sometimes form in the eyewall.

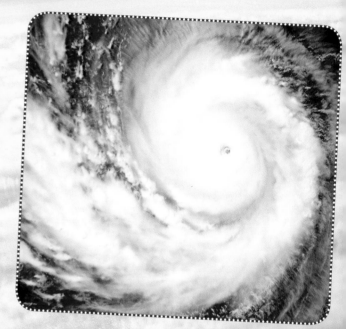

Hurricane Bonnie in 1998 was twice as tall as Mount Everest, the highest mountain on Earth.

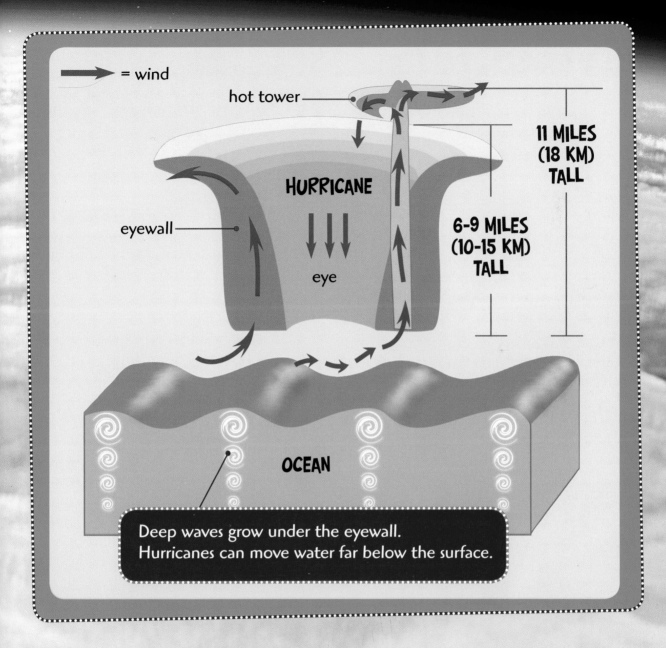

Hot towers can be more than 11 miles (18 km) tall. These tall clouds are warmer and wetter than the air around them. They make hurricanes even stronger.

DESTRUCTION

Hurricanes that hit land cause great damage.

As much as 40 inches (102 centimeters) of rain may fall.

Winds blow sideways. They tear roofs off buildings. The winds may last for many hours or even days.

The winds die down. But the storm is not over. The hurricane's eye is passing over. The calm may last a few hours.

"THE HUDSON RIVER CAME IN AND FILLED HALF OF HOBOKEN LIKE A BATHTUB."

—Mayor Dawn Zimmer of Hoboken, New Jersey, after Superstorm Sandy flooded the city in 2012

A deep wave called a storm surge hits the coast. The waves can be as tall as 20 feet (6 meters). Floods wash over the land and damage buildings.

HURRICANE SEASONS

Hurricane season is long in the Northern Hemisphere. It lasts for more than half of the year.

North America

NORTHEASTERN PACIFIC OCEAN
most hurricanes occur mid-May–November

NORTHERN ATLANTIC OCEAN
most hurricanes occur June–November

equator

South America

SOUTHERN PACIFIC OCEAN
most hurricanes occur January–March

Ocean waters must be at least 82 degrees Fahrenheit (28 degrees Celsius) for hurricanes to form.

Europe

Asia

NORTHWESTERN PACIFIC OCEAN
most hurricanes occur June–December

Africa

SOUTHERN INDIAN OCEAN
most hurricanes occur January–March

Australia

Hurricane season in the Southern Hemisphere happens during the other half of the year.

WHAT'S IN A NAME?

ATLANTIC NAMES

2014	2015	2016	2017	2018	2019
Arthur	Ana	Alex	Arlene	Alberto	Andrea
Bertha	Bill	Bonnie	Bret	Beryl	Barry
Cristobal	Claudette	Colin	Cindy	Chris	Chantal
Dolly	Danny	Danielle	Don	Debby	Dorian
Edouard	Erika	Earl	Emily	Ernesto	Erin
Fay	Fred	Fiona	Franklin	Florence	Fernand
Gonzalo	Grace	Gaston	Gert	Gordon	Gabrielle
Hanna	Henri	Hermine	Harvey	Helene	Humberto
Isaias	Ida	Ian	Irma	Isaac	Ingrid
Josephine	Joaquin	Julia	Jose	Joyce	Jerry
Kyle	Kate	Karl	Katia	Kirk	Karen
Laura	Larry	Lisa	Lee	Leslie	Lorenzo
Marco	Mindy	Matthew	Maria	Michael	Melissa
Nana	Nicholas	Nicole	Nate	Nadine	Nestor
Omar	Odette	Otto	Ophelia	Oscar	Olga
Paulette	Peter	Paula	Philippe	Patty	Pablo
Rene	Rose	Richard	Rina	Rafael	Rebekah
Sally	Sam	Shary	Sean	Sara	Sebastien
Teddy	Teresa	Tobias	Tammy	Tony	Tanya
Vicky	Victor	Virginie	Vince	Valerie	Van
Wilfred	Wanda	Walter	Whitney	William	Wendy

The first storm each season starts with an A.
Each storm continues through the alphabet.
The names switch between girl and boy names.

NORTHEASTERN PACIFIC NAMES

2014	2015	2016	2017	2018	2019
Amanda	Andres	Agatha	Adrian	Aletta	Alvin
Boris	Blanca	Blas	Beatriz	Bud	Barbara
Cristina	Carlos	Celia	Calvin	Carlotta	Cosme
Douglas	Dolores	Darby	Dora	Daniel	Dalila
Elida	Enrique	Estelle	Eugene	Emilia	Erick
Fausto	Felicia	Frank	Fernanda	Fabio	Flossie
Genevieve	Guillermo	Georgette	Greg	Gilma	Gil
Hernan	Hilda	Howard	Hilary	Hector	Henriette
Iselle	Ignacio	Isis	Irwin	Ileana	Ivo
Julio	Jimena	Javier	Jova	John	Juliette
Karina	Kevin	Kay	Kenneth	Kristy	Kiko
Lowell	Linda	Lester	Lidia	Lane	Lorena
Marie	Marty	Madeline	Max	Miriam	Manuel
Norbert	Nora	Newton	Norma	Norman	Narda
Odile	Olaf	Orlene	Otis	Olivia	Octave
Polo	Patricia	Paine	Pilar	Paul	Priscilla
Rachel	Rick	Roslyn	Ramon	Rosa	Raymond
Simon	Sandra	Seymour	Selma	Sergio	Sonia
Trudy	Terry	Tina	Todd	Tara	Tico
Vance	Vivian	Virgil	Veronica	Vicente	Velma
Winnie	Waldo	Winifred	Wiley	Willa	Wallis
Xavier	Xina	Xavier	Xina	Xavier	Xina
Yolanda	York	Yolanda	York	Yolanda	York
Zeke	Zelda	Zeke	Zelda	Zeke	Zelda

flood after Hurricane Katrina

The name list is reused every six years. However, a name is removed from the list if a storm by that name causes a lot of damage. For instance, Sandy and Katrina have both been removed from the names list.

FAMOUS HURRICANES

GREAT GALVESTON HURRICANE

In September 1900 a strong hurricane hit Galveston, Texas. At least 6,000 people died.

HURRICANE KATRINA

In August 2005 a weak hurricane passed over Florida.

It grew stronger as it moved over the Gulf of Mexico to Louisiana and Mississippi.

Heavy floods swept over the city of New Orleans. About 80 percent of the city flooded. More than 1,800 people died.

high-water mark

SUPERSTORM SANDY

Hurricane Sandy began in October 2012. It first hit islands in the Caribbean.

As it traveled north, a cold storm met it. It grew into a superstorm that hit the northeastern United States. The storm caused $65 billion dollars in damage.

Hurricane Sandy was 900 miles (1,448 km) across.

FAMOUS CYCLONES

CYCLONE BHOLA

In 1970 one of the deadliest storms in history hit East Pakistan (now called Bangladesh).

A storm surge flooded crowded cities.

As many as 500,000 people died.

CYCLONE TRACY

Cyclone Tracy struck Darwin, Australia, on Christmas Eve 1974. Winds blew at 155 miles (249 km) per hour.

Many did not listen to warnings because of the holiday.

Most people in the town lost their homes. People rebuilt stronger homes.

CYCLONE NARGIS

A strong cyclone hit Myanmar (also called Burma) in May 2008. Nargis blew over the land for two days.

At least 138,000 people died. Many people were never found.

STUDYING HURRICANES

Meteorologists use satellites in space to watch for hurricanes.

They watch how a storm moves. They learn how strong it will be.

Telling where the storm will travel is very important.

Aircraft with special equipment fly into hurricanes.

They drop instruments into the eyewall and eye. The instruments measure wind speeds and gather other information.

Radios send the information to meteorologists.

Warnings help people stay safe.

GETTING READY

Anyone who lives in a hurricane path should be ready.

People sometimes put boards over windows to protect them.

Listen carefully to warnings.

Go to a shelter or other safe place if your area must evacuate.

Hurricanes can last about a week.

When they hit land, they become weaker.

Without warm ocean water to power a hurricane, it blows away.

People work hard to clean up the mess left behind.

GLOSSARY

air pressure—the weight of air on a surface

clockwise—turning in the direction of the hands on a clock

counterclockwise—turning the opposite direction of the hands on a clock

cyclone—a hurricane that occurs in the southwestern Pacific or Indian oceans

evacuate—to leave an area during a time of danger

eye—a calm circle in the middle of a hurricane

eyewall—the area circling the eye of a hurricane; winds are strongest and rain is heaviest here

hemisphere—half of Earth

meteorologist—a person who studies and predicts the weather

satellite—a spacecraft that circles Earth; satellites gather and send information to Earth

shelter—a safe place where people can stay during a disaster

storm surge—a sudden, strong rush of water that happens as a hurricane moves onto land

superstorm—a hurricane that joins with another storm system; superstorms are extremely destructive

tropical—near the equator

tropical depression—a medium-sized storm over the ocean near the equator; the winds are between 23 to 38 miles (37 to 61 km) per hour

tropical disturbance—a small storm that forms over the ocean near the equator; winds are up to 22 miles (35 km) per hour

typhoon—a hurricane that occurs in the northwestern Pacific Ocean

CRITICAL THINKING USING THE COMMON CORE

Read about air pressure on page 7. What does the word "pressure" mean? What clues can you find in the text to help you? (Craft and Structure)

Look at the the photo labels on pages 10 and 11. What is the scientific name for the hole of the doughnut? Why do you think it is called that? (Key Ideas and Details)

The label on page 22 explains that the stripes on the house are high-water marks. Why do you think there is more than one stripe? (Integration of Knowledge and Ideas)

READ MORE

Aboff, Marcie. *Hurricanes!* First Graphics: Wild Earth. Mankato, Minn.: Capstone Press, 2012.

Gibbons, Gail. *Hurricanes!* New York: Holiday House, 2009.

Gonzales, Doreen. *Hurricanes*. Killer Disasters. New York: PowerKids Press, 2013.

INTERNET SITES

FactHound offers a safe, fun way to find Internet sites related to this book. All of the sites on FactHound have been researched by our staff.

Here's all you do:

Visit *www.facthound.com*

Type in this code: 9781476539324

Check out projects, games and lots more at
www.capstonekids.com

INDEX